A special thanks to my incredible loved ones who have
supported my writing throughout all of these years.
You are my inspiration and muse.

And to you, reader, that you might find strange
connection and beauty between our human experience.

Written & Illustrated
By
Mariah Neumaier

Sleepwalker

A swan
And the dripping shower drain is my best friend
Grinding eternity's soft face into rug burn
Hair whispers secrets into the feathers of a downy pillow
Watching intently every evening
As the remainder spills from the skull like a tea spout
Moistens a dream with tasteless poison
Shallow slices in the windowsill
Spell out a pitiful jargon
Only the deathbed can translate
Rising slowly for a last smirking remark
The bitter spit of fate
A moment outside of the skin
I wasn't finished

Driving is as easy as Drowning

Cars dancing
Man-made metal slugs
Fading in the orange bask
Of a fallen sun
My eyes grope the scene, drink it in.
Conglomeration of beating hearts
Traveling to the arms of an awaiting affair
Perhaps to pick up more damn diapers from the store
Or
Watching your sick decrepit uncle slip away
I believe that they are searching for something of relevance
In a world of simple functions and complex circumstances

When I was young, I always wanted a carport on my house.
To study the rain falling in blankets around me.
Two inches from my fingertips, and I am dry.
Two feet and I could find myself laying on the flooding pavement,
Water rushing into my nostrils
Plastering my hair through the rubble.

Why is it that I observe from afar, amazed by it?
Cinch back my finger as if rain will sizzle on it
Grease on a cherry red stove

We are people afraid of the things we cannot explain
Moments we cannot conceptualize
Without expert terms and inches
Without multiple cylinder engines and lobular diagrams

Thoughts that drop off our tongues like saliva
Before the words even begin to form

Call me a vehicle of transcendence
Window watching the moments that pass me
Upon opening the forbidden portal to the outside
To the rain
And the water permeates the dry compartment

We are not one without cataclysm

M-16 Sleeping Soundly on Your Neck

The indigo shadow
Hanging like earrings from behind
The soft skin of your neck
Licks you with stiff nostalgia

You lay heavy on the sticks
Water rising
Like a bath
Spine sinking in soft mud
And the carcasses of cartridges
Sprinkling like splendid
Stars

Funny how we all just keep on living
Somewhere inside of a straight jacket once
Our palms separate from the clay

The blackening of the vine
Wilting, weak, one last berry clings
Explosion onto your dry tongue
You lick the remnants off your unclean fingers
And weep

When nothing else, Gravity holds me

One thousand and eighty days, Love.
Robbed clean with a
Bathtub baptism

Brass bracelet rusting
Satin drawers, drawers, drawers.

Falling for the second of
One, maybe three?
Three.
And a set of lips on the collarbone
Under the cracked moon

Our names are carved into the wood splintering
Of a pond pier
Cockeyed bike helmet
Two sizes too big

Recollection; sensational impressions

With a friendly caterpillar's
Slinking green follicles
Stiffening antennae
On the lap
Of a pleated plaid jumper

With a handful of pyrite
Fingers grasping uncaught minnows
Glistening muddy treasures
The captive fragments among
Rainwater in a hose bucket

With sliced star fruit shaking
Crumpled plastic baggie
Crushed to the bottom of a denim backpack
Mallard duck handle
On a day umbrella

With knees firmly rooted
Into the grouted ground
Bass trembling porcelain
Brief discussion of combustion
Copper paperweight
Echoes the seductive neck
Of a pistol

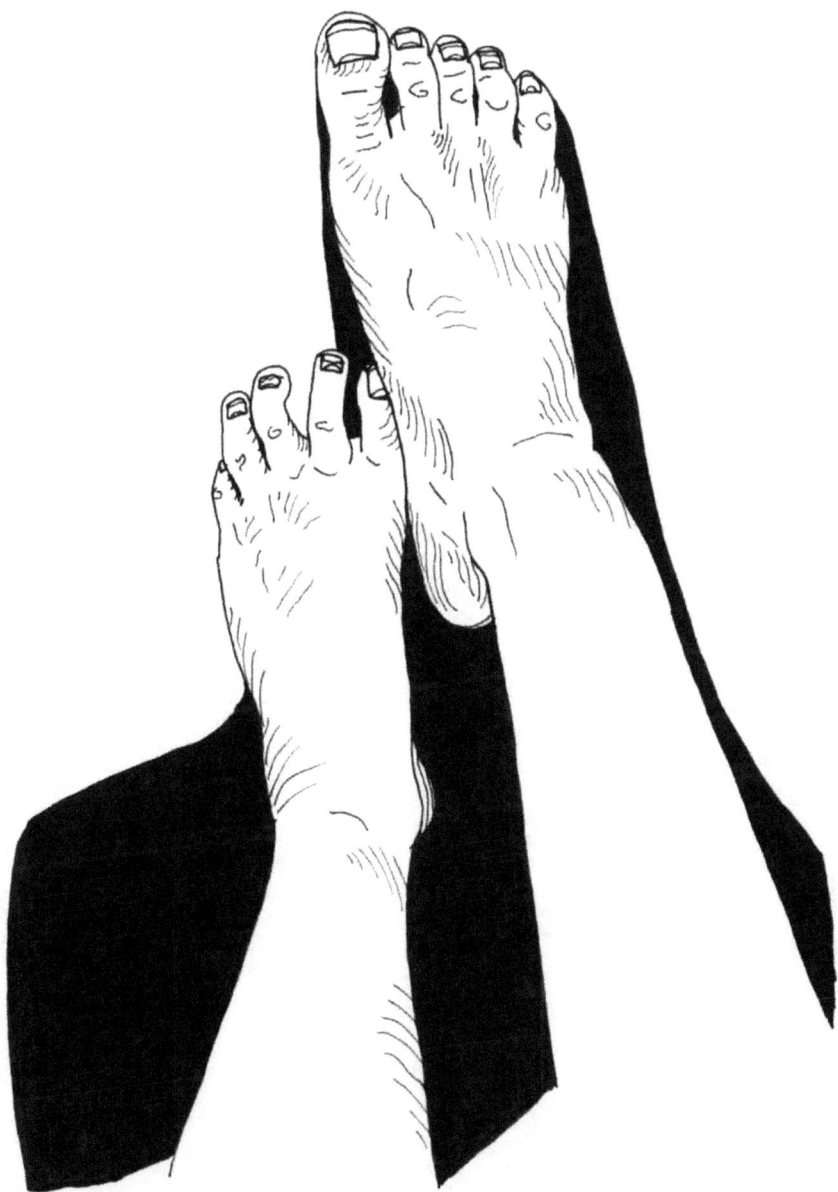

Memory's Garden

Prized peach bathroom
With soaps shaped like sea shells
Dissolved into the soft folding glove of wrinkled fingers

Crouching to touch the soil before mass
Hidden whispering communes by the corner fence
Behind an empty pool
Roots that ardently cling to oxygen
        The bleeding hearts are blooming

Glow pours from the mouth, a lighthouse in Maine
Foaming waves spit salt into the furious atmosphere
And the frogs are singing their love song
Funneling into the pale cone that strikes the sky

Stars are headlights on the rain-slicked highway
Tasteless thoughts that vaporize
Off spinning tires
Suffocate under the severed eyelash
Of an April crescent

Half past three

The deep grumbling vibrations of insomnia
That carve themselves deep ridges into the lingering
The ceiling fan is whipping a tornado
The soft fluttering of unanchored pages
Feathers of half written love letters
Melancholic poems
Or maybe suicide notes
That hide in the dog eared safes of book collections
Dusty little empires among the upper shelf of an untouched library

Maybe I was meant to be a sixty five year old alcoholic
Getting drunk on Shiraz and dancing to scratched records
In striped culottes

A mind cannot forget the flushed skin under an office lamp
Filled with glorious tears and swollen strawberry lips
I liked you in the wash of the old tv that sang an eerie hiss

I think a lot about the way we suffer
Finding anecdotal quotes to re-digest
Sickeningly bright yellow lacquer over all the imperfect bits

I loved you deep into the night you never knew
Or failed to keep alive in your existence

Reptilian

I have a heart of red felt
Red like carmine rubies in your great grandmothers wedding ring
Or depitted cherries soaking in the remains of juice
Or maybe my heart is bread that crumbles
Between your teeth

The tempestuous lies of a saccharine tongue
Entice me faster than the cast iron gates
Of my garden can bar in the safety
Of blossoming buds
To the trampling sneaker of a reckless child
Searching for his frisbee lodged among the fragile lily of the valley

I'm kept up at night by the sound of pumping
That accompanies my left nipple
And the gesture of ghastly torture when I think of your wrists and lips
As they congregate on puckered pores

    The sweet scent of honeysuckle
    And rotting fruit

Laying under the dining room table
Scrawled markings and staples from the warehouse it slept in
Lace partitions
And the shined patent leather loafers
Next to my mothers white satin mules
Her burgundy toe nail polish is chipped
Grab her pinky toe and she swats at me like a fly over her hidden lap

I wait for you like I wait for that lashing pat at my frizzed strands

Anticipation that hangs low like breasts
As the shower tiles heat with steam
I wait for a beating
A beating of a slinging clawed palm
A beating of an affection tickled artery

Sanpaku

The palm heart protected by the mirrored lull of plastic fronds
Paling pink of a Pentecostal church in St. John
Double rows of pearly washing machine teeth
Bubbling of feathers in the thickening suds
And the parrots are somewhere cackling, afraid
A power washer is skinning the raw porcelain of a fountain
Permanent settlements
Time has spread her wings
Over Little Rock motel
Here the Japanese maple petrified in lichen
Electrified
Everywhere known peered at the same smirk of moon

"You could hop up and ride that cloud to Florida"

Fallen night's trembling fingernails
Brush through the arms of mighty oak trees
And into the veins of moss that crawl through ruptured concrete

Captive newspapers are molding in the edging banks that cave up
To find the soles I stand my weight upon

Gingerbread mansions are lit up like forgotten candles in the dawning
Lonesome saturation on the leery edges;
Her phosphorescent border
I make it out of squinted irises, the near-sided moons of fleeting midnight
She curls fernlike, a fetus at the foot palms of the universe

Close my impish eyes to feel the voice
The cracked light of morning,
Her coaxing thumbs push through dusk to find
Two cardinals flirting in a pine tree

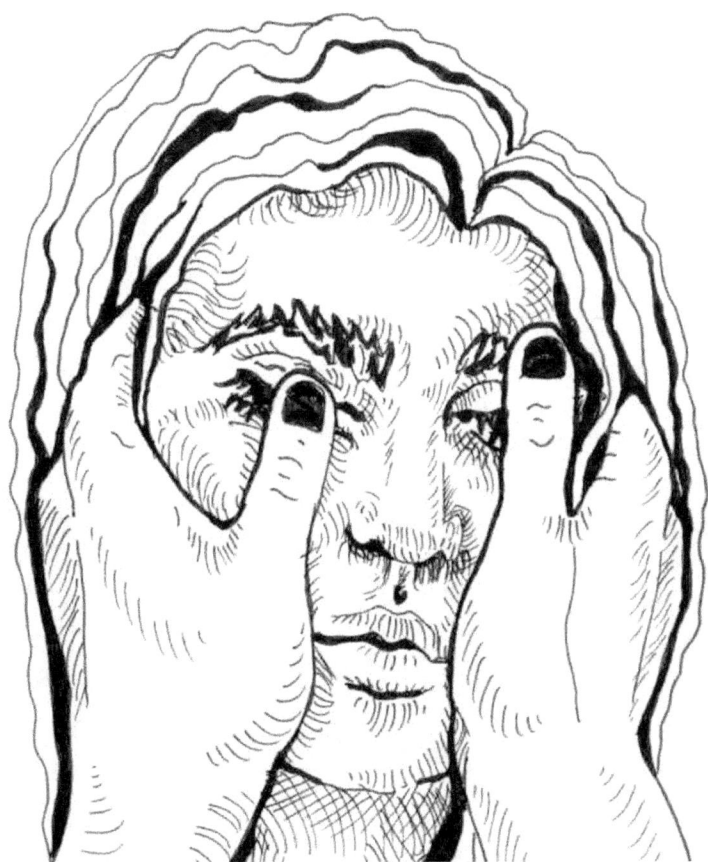

Dry mouth

Grey and the thigh of a flirting atmosphere bares
Fleshy stars through fishnets

A smile hangs to foreign lips
Like the string of ornament

Douglass Fir that sprouts against
The glassy window of a laced pane
All frosted in the white dressing with the purity of a bride
Her sickly fingers that trace the shaking tree bones
Bring on a burning comfort
Subsides quite nicely on a chilled twilight

The refrigerated bottle of white wine
Sweating in the heat of a crystal dining chandelier
Hangs low above the brows of unkempt silence
Two lovers in their historic secrets
The fizzling parts too heavily unrevealed
The rice paper partition that blossoms
Into the cool veins of a white marble wall
And they sink like snow into the late February

My Dad's Song

A song that lies somewhere in the entrenched reefs of a lake in Michigan
Where the wind blows strong and cold
A ruffling in the lace of a wedding train
Alphabet soup spells out a will
Two books of Cummings and a poisonous sulfite rock

And I think it brings him out there in the May
Digging handfuls of garden into the waist of his collared shirt.
Flowers by the belly button still moist with rainwater.

Wood is interchangeable with granite, depending on how you play it.
Resting under the posy holders and sprouts a pansy from the diluted ashes.
She waits for him as he sleeps

The butterflies of midnight that flit through the dulling wash of stars
They seek the lively gardens they once belonged to before dusk settled
Heavy blankets are sun shades over warm chocolate eyes
A song buried in the soil

One Trick Pony

Blue breath
Sticking like gum
To ozone
How does it feel, Friend
Against the tender rims of nostrils?

Wade through clouds of sickly
Acetone sweats
Putrid scents slithering
Thick honey dripping
Chapped, Chalked, Choked

Ashes scatter across grasses
Sand mounds in a play box
Wind of laughter tangles
Whistling through a deviated septum

Mama fractured her china pitcher
And a balding tabby cat
Lapped up lakes of cream
With a bleeding tongue

.

Baby

Nine travel size bottles of mouthwash
Lay discarded under the kitchen sink
Behind the rolls of pristine paper towels
We found her shaking in fetal position
Naked and zipped into the bright green
Suitcase you brought each year to Indiana
For business
Her eyes were beady and lips a sickly blue
She reached out with a clammy grasp
As if to tell me something
But the words were lost on her tongue

It was better when she was drinking whiskey
And laid in bed all day
Staring at the burgundy wall
With a fixed and yet somehow distant gaze
A sophisticated color that she dreamt of
As a young house wife
Now, it made her sick with despair
It was an accident, really, that I saw her through the crack
In the double doors
She repeated the same phrase again and again
Tomorrow I will start over

Tomorrow she will have her hair curled
And pinned about her shoulders with a blush painted
High and bright on her hollowed cheekbones
An intoxicating smile

Waiting patiently to slip away
To her secrets
Hidden amongst the Christmas ornaments
Under the front seat of her car
Inside the box that holds her lace wedding dress

And once the house is empty
She will find herself sitting in it
Ballooning around her
A pure white chrysanthemum
And watch with intense fascination
As she loses herself inside the handle.

Sometimes with her hair slicked back
Eyes scrambling and inebriated
She can nearly identify
The same soft stare of the precocious ten year old
Admiring herself in her neighbors vanity mirror
Swallow perched from the walnut tree
Long before her husband forgot to remind her
That she was beautiful

Into her own gaze
She whispers, fingers fondling
The pearl beading that surrounds
What once were her young virgin breasts,
Tomorrow I will start over

Close Set of Three Threads

Three closely hung black blazers
Sit in a grieving set
Behind the white doors
Of my closet
Not a singular touch of dust
Singes the angular hem
They lay lazy on wood hangers
Imminent moment
Unfolding itself
In no less than a minute
Clock
tick tick tock
Emulates the sound
Of a clicking lock
Pull open the heavy handles
With a heaving sigh
Cloak my shoulders
With the emblazoned
Jacket

Following Fury like the North Star

Soundless whispers in the dead of night
Our mind holds onto with concentrated might
It is never what you think it is
A dim glow, a dull fizz.

Tonight all of your past lovers
Are somewhere sleeping under separate covers
Breathlessly drawn to cheap excuses
The shocking sockets, burnt out fuses.

Extract the pulp of the matter
The glass that will surely shatter
With citrus concentrate on fingertips
Warped wood hugging sunken ships.

Spice that inflames the lips
And ice for the bleeding hips
Pregnant mind, laborious intoxication
Unfiltered conversation, tongue's laceration.

Swimming in the weighty depths of sea,
Searching minds for nobody, with no body,
Irrelevant fear, the inner voice is irreverent
As sure as sunset, such becomes evident.

Twenty Three Seconds, Arriving at Destination

Smeared baby hairs to your crisp collar
Curling up with a keen, fringed edge

The desolate parking lot

To meet with you under buzzing fluorescents
Aflame in the blackness
And we swap sweat from trembling palms
And we do not let go quickly enough

Unable to avoid electric shears buzzing
Through severed nerve endings
And now the bones are dislocated
Through the papery skin of equanimity

So what now, you say
Clenched purpled jaw
Dead end questions
That it damns back

Clammy hands against
Dry denim pant pockets
A tempted sinner reaching for
The quenching holy word
Of a merciful spirit

Waiting that crawls under stockings
Raising spikes with perpetual itching
Choking on the coldness with crushed lungs
And a crinkling whisper

Wake up for me

Stay here with me, she's pleads
It's time, he gurgles
Dribble down his slack jaw
Moldy damp basement
And the weight of two bodies
On the beat up beanbag chair

Many times this has been
And now is a changing moment
Blood and glass crushed in the palms of hands
Caressing the face of a shattered mirror
Moments protruding cantilever
Into the languishing unknown of existence
Staring into the silent barrel of breathing, beating

Watching with flecks of promise
Puncture the same choking hope
In the rainy car before he blurted
I'm going to stop
I promise you, I'm going to stop

Watching in a daze, inebriated homeless man
Twisting on a skateboard in the dancing rain
Falls hard on his ass in shrill laughter
He lay on his back in the pooling
No movement
Hollow throat occluding

Loving After the Unclean Touch

A mere blink in the abysmal drudge of pattern.
Intimacy has become a rare scintillation
In a stale existence

The entropy of devotion
Pleasure lives companionless when reduced to flesh
A diorama
Romance inside of the golden rectangle
Is enslaved to the eyes of a pervert

Persephone with crimson juice on her lips
Seals her fate

The bony fingers pry petals
Killing daisies in a queer attempt to measure
Whether your sweaty lover
Thinks fondly of the cryptic slope
Of eyes you borrowed from your father

Modern woman using skin as tissues
Obsidian wave of silk blankets the fury
Sewn into your chest

Warm emphasis presses
His toes into your stomach pit
As ruddy blush pools

To welcome and suffer
Both the entirety and oblivion
Sweated
And Wept
By the same lungs
Tongue and blood
That your specter is captive of

The essence is exhausted
Trapped underneath heavy water

A sacrifice to taste the bright ruby jewel
Only to find rusty copper
A lackluster bubble to the surface
Then dissipating all at once in the frontal lobe

Unwound Casette Tape

I'll never forget the smell of rain
at my father's funeral
and the way you saw me.
Your eyes sunken and grey.
How when drunk, you snickered
And wittily retorted, beer
dripping onto the
pastel flowers of my neckline
from your lips.

There were nights laying
across my mattress,
phone cord coiled
around my finger
like a ring
grinning at the secrets
You
whispered into my
willing ears.
And later
Across the same sheets
I swam in perspiration.
Wondering where
you were and
who
you were doing.

You're the only man
Whose touch
I have trusted.

Syncopation

And then the aleatory quality of freckles
Splashing into the pale of crushed velvet

The sweetest delicacies sour slowly
Darkness seeping steadily into the bleed
Affection is sleeping
Trepidation is breathing
Cursed marriage of completion and fracture

Skin that curls around the bones in
Sharp grotesque fashions
Organic curves interrupted by
Black ink diffusing around the edges

Never-ending trickle of exuberance
Sunken decay of exhalation
Bent by the sigh of the cycle
Blows stoutly into hollow chests
And then with shocking force
Siphons us empty

Universe's Galactic Foil

The prayer of a silver Buick's swan song
Sliding across slick pavement
Our mother gaurdrail cups soft skin upon impact
A moment swims with deep feeling

The destructive nature of life
Holds tightly to the moments of purity
The core of our foundational strength roots itself
In nicotine rolls between freshly waxed lips
The scents of similar nights with one's first love

We are learning to swim in the cotton of peaked sheets
And valleys that wander between carves and toes
My religion is kindness and tenderness
And the simplicity of felicity
Before it melts

Anoint me with Anise and Tequila

The perfect banana
Is always a little too ripe
My flesh
Itches to wear it's appointed tomb of skin
Unapologetically

How does one properly soak the soft smile of your lips
In their holiness
Lou Reed's magic moment

And afterwards all that's left
Is sand in the bottom of your loafers
          How perturbing!

Drink in the musky scents of the morning pillow
Cradling a head in the dark
Left only to hypothesize
          Which way the earth is turning today
And which arms you long after with innocent wonder
                    When your slumbered eyes wrinkle

You'd certainly be the most dog-eared book I owned

Bug Bite

Lay amidst the scratching thistle,
Accompanied by a pesky cricket's whistle,
Fabricated world for a lonely soul to live in,
Just a grave of sardines in a metal tin.

Greyness thickens, thickens by the hour
Horses whine and the blazing sun is sour

Woken with a suffocating fear
Darkness is an ever-shrinking atmosphere
A caterpillar stepped into the warm mud
Petals torn away from the tightly knit bud

Three fingers up to shield my eyes
I am being told a dirty joke by the flies